AF410091

This is the revised version of the the seconf editiion of the Enigma Of Poetry-Volume One.

The picture overleaf is about Lake Malawi, one of the ten largest kakes in the world. It is the freshwater lake. It has the rare species of fish called Chambo. it is the very tasty fish.

THE ENIGMA OF POETRY

VOLUME ONE

THIRD EDITION

DEDICATIONS

This poetic book has been dedicated to my beloved wife, Mafuno Malemia and my beloved son, Moses Malemia.

TABLE OF CONTENTS

TABLE OF CONTENTS

INTRODUCTION

The Enigma Of Poetry-Volume One is a poetic book consisting of poems of various types. The types are as follows:

Spiritual Issues: This document is portraying the issues of spirituality. It is talking about how you should attain the status of Christianity. This starts by believing in Jesus Christ and accepting and accepting Him as one's personal Saviour.

We are living in the world of conflicting choices.

Nature: Some poems are expressing the issues of the creation of nature and the human impact on mother nature with her reciprocal consequences.

Human personalities and behaviours:These are being featured in certain poetic pieces. They are both bad and good personalities or behaviours.

The journey through life: The journey through life is unforeseeable.

We pass through hard and pleasant situations. All in all, we should give thanks to GOD ALMIGHTY for the precious gift of life which He gives us daily. We should learn to enjoy our life continually despite having several challenges along our respective destinies.

This has been just to mention a few of the issues this book hold.

Read, underatand, enjoy and share the information therein.

Thanks

THE LONG AWAITED DAY HAS COME!

Praised be the LORD for this day;
Let HIS name be magnified;
Let HIM have our daily bread satisfied;
Praised be HIM always.

Suddenly, heard I, tinkling sounds from the kitchen;
Women had to hasten;
Cleaning the utensils;
In place were vessels;
To be used by invited guests;
Who were to appreciate different tastes.

Men were chopping wood;
Talking were some and others stood;
Laughter crackled;
Excitement quaked.

What a great scenario?
A day of feast was in style;
Music was sounding;
Comedies, jokes, energizers, e.t.c.
were a moment worth founding.

It is a time for a quarrel;
Sleep and excitement were parallel;
Rest and eagerness were conflicting;
Eyelids were heavy and afflicting.

Eventually, nature took charge;

For none had to grudge;

Everyone went to sleep;

The great scenario had come to an end.

GENEROSITY

What is generosity?
Why is it present in our society?
How is it attained?
Where can it be obtained?

Always ready to give out whole heartedly;
A generous person acts flexible mindedly;
Genuine generosity is a component of love;
Makes, it, the world to move round.

Equitable resource distribution is targeted;
The give and get blessed formula is in it fitted;
Fame and riches are its products;
Intentional/conditional generosity isn't a good conduct.

Self confidence and satisfaction are in the owner;
Increases, it, knowledge, wealth with honor;
It is unconditional, empathetic and innovative;
It acts patiently and is active.

It is like a basket in drought of fortunes;
Which can be filled up at the time opportune;
It can be inherited or inherent;
It can be acquired;
A tool, it is, in good personality.

I PRAISE YOU MY LORD

Waking up in the morning;
As the day is dawning;
I should praise YOU;
For the breath of life due.

With an unimaginable diligence;
YOUR word endures with resilience;
By YOUR mighty hand;
YOU formed the sea and land.

Praise, praise HIM always;
Our protector and guide in many ways;
Praise HIM in singing;
Glorify HIM in dancing.

Praised be YOU forever;
As YOU are my savior;
MAKER of universe YOU are;
I praise YOU my LORD.

GROPING FOR CHRIST

In dire need of CHRIST I am;
A searcher for HIM I become;
Elusive HE is;
To those in disbelief and sin.

With my physical efforts, I labor;
Still in vain, missing HIS splendor;
Too religiously, I act;
As if it is the only fact.

How is this KING found?
Where is HE?
What proceeds from HIS finding?
Several questions proceed from my mind.

Believe in HIS resurrection from the dead;
You will be saved by HIM;
At the right hand of the throne of HIS FATHER;
You will be set free.

OUR GOD IS A GREAT ARTIST

YOUR prowess in next to none;
YOUR word created the sun;
The universe is YOUR hand's work;
YOUR voice makes the earth to shake.

Man was created in YOUR own image;
All the earthly nature was laid on him to manage;
Man was given dominion over the earth;
But his sin provoked confusion and death.

Adam and Eve, why did you sin?
Sin has produced various troubles we are seeing;
They range from wars, diseases to hatred;
But the sin healing blood of JESUS is sacred.

The sea, wind and whole nature obey JESUS;
HIS HOLY SPIRIT should always be in us;
It leads us to everlasting life;
Our ways and deeds should be right.

Our GOD, really, is a great artist;
Let HIS name be exalted and everlasting;
The whole universe is bound in YOUR words;
The universe is the product of HIS work.

Let YOUR name be blessed forever.

HIV

I'm HIV;
A threat to lives;
Incurably, I persist;
For none can resist.

I attack, mostly, reckless people;
Who look down upon me as simple;
I've got several entry routes;
Sex, transplacental, to me, they suit;
Others are exchange of sharp/pointed objects;
Blood transfusion, also, to concerned subjects.

I'm a victor against bodily armies;
Antibodies are their names;
Their gradual weakening is my policy;
Their defeat is without partiality.

ARV has tried my elimination;
In me, he meets enormous determination;
To cause havoc to health, economy;
And expected human sociology.

Two enemies murder my sleep;
Lest they lead me to a heavy slip;
Firsly, preventive measures are being offered;
Finally, Anti HIV vaccine is in the offing;
But! Still I am the king!!!

SUPPLICATION

Let's obey the LORD whole heartedly;
And follow the WORD single mindedly;
Begging for abundant mercies and grace;
Waiting for their realization at a pace.

Let's pray for our needs, hard;
As fasting should always be at hand;
Let's give generously to the poor;
As the sweet smelling oil that pour.

Let's intercede for the needs of others;
As we are one body of CHRIST altogether;
For in unity there is strength;
Leading to love of greater depth.

Our sole purpose is for HIS glorification;
WHO is blameless and our purification;
Through the process of supplication;
We acquire sanctification.

BACK TO SCHOOL

Preparing for a new academic year;
A learner makes everything clear;
To the guardian to think over;
And arrange for the costs to cover.

I'm back to school;
The environment is calm and cool;
Foretelling good learning period;
With my fellows, both inferior and superior.

Suddenly, occur the changes;
Tough going, is the order in exchange;
Piles of notes and assignments recur;
Causing panic, about everything, to recall.

Back to school, really, I'm;
Forgetting about the home and farm;
Serious business is my motto;
For concentration to be total.

This is sports time;
Announces the prefect on line;
Exams come;
Excellent results become;
Back to school, really, I like.

CHENJERANI

Chenjerani anthu inu;
Woyipayo anadza m'dziko lino;
Iye ndiye tate wa bodza;
Woyipa ngati mfiti yolodza.

Mpeweni anthu inu;
Valani zida zonse za Chikhristu;
Kuti mupatuke misampha yake;
Imene ayitchera mopanda ubale.

Musacheukenso anthu inu;
Chamchere, mungadzasanduke chulu;
Ngati mayi Loti potuluka m'Sodomu;
Woyipaya wadzadza ndi machimo katamu.

Mtamandeni Leza, anthu inu;
Ndi mwana wake, Yesu;
Mwazi wake umachotsa machimo;
Amene anthu timadzipatsa nawo ntchito.

Mtulireni mabvuto, anthu inu;
Goli lanu lidzapepukatu;
Popeza IYE ndi njira, choonadi ndi moyo;
Umene udzakhala wa muyaya.

Chimwemwe chidzakhala nanu;
Mtendere udzakhala ngodya yake;
Umenewu udzakhala mpaka ku Paradizo;
Mzimu Woyera, mwa inu, ulamulire maganizo;
Chenjerani anthu inu.

HUMILITY

The character regards itself lowly;
It acts and thinks slowly;
It is not puffed up;
It puts itself last and others up.

Obediently, statutes and standards are followed;
Never despises, for no cause its neighbours;
Patient, it is;
Inborn or acquired, it is.

Leads, it, to an effective leader;
It does not possess jealousy of others;
Perfect social interaction proceeds from it;
It is extrovert and altruistic.

It is termed humility;
An important tool in good personality;
It is a component of love;
It is indispensable to have.

COMPANIONSHIP WITH CHRIST

Loneliness is biting me hard;
I am like a house without guard;
Several issues through my mind lingers
Swirling emotions occur, but never wither;
What methods should deliver the goods?

Is it a result of homophobia?
Is it a consequence of fear?
Is it a proceed of selfishness?
Is it really a product of sin?
I send an S.O.S. for assistance.

Companionship! Companionship is its resolution;
Social security will come into evolution;
Stable personality will be achieved;
Fear will be thrown into mental archive;
Selfishness will appear no more.

Oh! COMPANION! I accept YOU whole heartedly;
YOU are a healing to my problem;
A cure to my emotions YOU are;
A remover of homophobia YOU are;
Fear run away from YOU;
Selfishness has no presence in YOUR place.

STREAKS OF DOUBTS

Streaks of doubts as a day breaks;
In my mind they linger and fade;
Turbulence, my heart feels;
With fear, my soul, fills.

My future, fuzzy vision, it holds;
My actions are frail and not bold;
Circumstances of me, advantages, they take;
Water tide, I resemble, at the lake.

Distress, my pillow, it becomes;
Depression, around me, never calms;
Nightmares, my daily vision, they are;
Streaks of doubts, as the day recurs.

My brethren, do not despair;
Your problem will be in repair;
Inquire of a sound vision;
Grope for wisdom and discretion.

You will have a sound judgment;
Your heart will store discernment;
Gladness and joy, your pillow, will be;
Streaks of confidence will ever be.

SOUND

How mysterious is sound?
It can be soft or hard;
Audible or inaudible, it can be;
It is heard, for none can see.

In three ways, it travels;
Through liquid, air, solid, to us, it marvels;
The ear is its natural antenna;
Its specialized structures are located internally.

How would soundless earth exist?
Would natural communication persist?
Safety of creatures would be endangered;
How mysterious is this energy when encountered?

Blessed be the CREATOR of sound;
As it is performing wonders along the ground;
Natural and artificial communications are enhanced;
Through it, distance is traced;
How mysterious is sound?

INDEED, YOU ARE WITH ME

Why am I still living?
Why are troubles being made lighter?
Why are all my needs being answered?

I hear YOUR still small voice;
To my needs it responds;
The problems being met are stepping stones;
To future greater heights of success, they lead.

Several mountains have been leveled;
Several depressions have been filled up;
YOU provide me with beautiful things;
Indeed, YOU are with me.

UNITY

Teach about unity;
Can it lead it to purity?
Which is the element of divinity;
As it is the basis of sanctity.

Please, teach me about unity;
Can it end up into sanity;
School about this difficulty;
Which is misleading in my society.

Teach me about unity;
Does it bring forth iniquity?
Or does it precede immorality?
Is it a precursor of enemity?

Alas! What is unity?
Is it about humility?
Which can result into generosity;
And leading to social prosperity.

Listen carefully my posterity;
I've a brief reply to your curiosity;
Unity is for both purity and iniquity;
It is strength in each extremity.

Pure unity is a social favorite;
Wicked unity is a social adversity;
Pure unity leads to meaningful frugality;
Wicked unity culminatea into social tragedy;
My posterity opt for pure unity.

NO NEED TO BE PROUD

Pride is self centred;
Pride is self seeking;
Pride exalts itself;
No need to be proud.

Hatred proceeds from it;
Social divisions are brought about;
It culminates into inefficient and ineffective resource distribution;
No need to be proud.

Pride is destructive;
Both subjectively and objectively;
It is commonplace;
No need to be proud.

Pride should be got rid of;
Disobedience to instructions to be switched off;
By following established statutes in the HOLY BOOK;
No need to be proud.

*E*NVIRONMENT

Environment is our surroundings;
Several, it has, the groupings;
Terrestrial, arboreal, celestial and aquatic;
Then it is made holistic.

Environment, degraded it is being;
Consequences we're seeing;
Pollution and climatic changes;
Lacking are alternatives in exchange.

Environment, indispensable, it is;
Ecosystems interrelate in it;
Nature is then maintained;
Then, it is sustained.

Environment, redressed, it can be;
Pollution and climatic changes can quit;
This is dreamed;
Which needs to be deemed;
Oh! Great damage! In environment!

JESUS FORGIVE ME

Deliberately, YOUR law, I flout;
Ignorantly, about YOUR power, I doubt;
Like a sheep, without a shepherd, I move;
About me, nothing righteous, for HIM to prove.

Thinking that I am great;
My ways are not straight;
Calamities, for me, they seek;
As anguish, with me, is.
Desperately, for solutions, I grope;
To remove calamities with hope;

Suddenly, of YOU, I reminisce;
Like a flash in minutes;
As a savior from my troubles;
Causing my sins, out, to bubble.
Please! JESUS forgive me!

CAUGHT BETWEEN CIRCUMSTANCES

Standing in the middle of nowhere;
Troubled, is my mind, to go somewhere;
Elusive, is the right direction, to search for;
Lest calamities, on me, could befall.

Tying up their knots while loosening others;
Like that, decisions patterns are, altogether;
Oh! My mother brain;
Lead me out of this trend.

To no avail, troubles around me, circumscribe;
Still caught between circumstances;
A victim of troubles, I persist;
As, no shield against them available, to resist.

Hoping for pending emancipation;
Still, ponders I, with anticipation;
To crack through this hard crust;
As the meek tongue breaks a bone;
Oh! Oh! Caught between circumstances, I am.

TEMPTATION! TEMPTATION!! TEMPTATION!!!

As a thorn, in my flesh, you exist;
For, in my society, you persist;
Irresistibly, yourself to me, you present;
From you, ways of your conquest, descend.

As common as air, you are;
For many experience your torture;
Temptation! Be careful!
My victory against you, will be aweful.

In endurable limits, your existence, is;
As the Holy Bible depicts it;
Jubilee in the day of your defeat;
As I will draw nearer to HIS SEAT.

Into pieces, cut you, will I;
With a sword, hold it, will I;
HIS holy word, it is;
As the dark world fears it.

Circumspectly, I will walk;
My feet, with the gospel of peace;
The helmet of salvation, my head being protected;
Breast plate of righteousness, on my chest, will be;
The belt of truth, around my waist, will be girded;
Against the wicked one, the shield of faith, will be;
Prayer and watchfulness shall also be;
Temptation! Leave me in advance!!

THE MYSTERY OF OUR GOD

Troubled, my mind is;
When, of natural mystery, I think;
To infinity, my imagination flows;
As unreachable and unsearchable extent of the universe.

How big and brief was HIS work plan;
Inconceivable was its span;
Natural component, together, fit perfectly;
As HE acts omnipotently.

What an infallible GOD we have?
The SUPERNATURAL BEING who saves;
Even those who hate HIM from danger;
Merciful, to them, is this MAKER.

Let my soul worship YOU;
Let my acts supplicate to YOU;
YOU deserve glory and honor;
For, abundantly, YOUR blessings pour;
Really, it's the mystery of our GOD.

I THANK YOU FOR THE RAIN DUE

Rain is falling in time;
From the ground, the seedlings rise;
To reach out for the sunlight;
Which provides energy for growth;
I thank YOU for the rain due.

Rain washes away waste;
Keeping the environment clean and safe;
Rain increases water table;
As water, through the ground, settles;
I thank YOU for the rain due.

Rain, in the water bodies, increases water level;
To be used for irrigation;
As flood brings alluvial soils to the banks;
Which improves soil fertility in the plains;
I thank YOU for the rain due.

Its formation, about it to think, is mysterious;
Signifying YOU are marvelous;
As it dissolves nutrients for plant usage;
Some of which derived from foliage;
I thank YOU for the rain due.

I HAVE FOUND YOU OUT

My dear lover;
My time for your waiting is over;
For I have found you;
At the moment due.

Loneliness hard, has bitten me;
A house without guard, I resembled;
Replaced rib, you are, in Eden;
As a helper in that garden.

My love as a ring is for you;
Unquenchable by water and dew;
Burning like fire;
Till death doeth us part.

My lover, let's be one;
Flesh of my flesh, bone of my bone;
To comply with Adam's formula;
Of leaving our respective family.

Let's, our future, work out;
After, our problems, we've found out;
Let's, in our society, make a difference;
Which is positive and with acceptance;
My dear lover, I have found you.

A POET USES POETRY, POETRY

Switching on the radio;
Stanzas being recited in style;
Skilled mouth uttered them swiftly;
For a poet uses poetry, poetry.

A flow of ideas;
Knitted into rhyming pairs;
Thought over patiently;
For a poet uses poetry, poetry.

What a valuable talent?
For issues both past and current;
Occurring violently or quietly;
For a poet uses poetry, poetry.

Teaching subjective or objective discernment;
To those thinking over them with judgment;
And consequently, acting discreetly;
For a poet uses poetry, poetry.

Contrary to anatomy;
Differing from astronomy;
Mainly related to sociology and psychology;
For a poet uses poetry, poetry.

I am a poet;
Having lingering issues in my mental bucket;
Which overflow perpetually;
For a poet uses poetry, poetry.

A MOUNTAIN TO COMMAND

A world of more questions than answers;
Ponders I as one of planners;
To rid of a quagmire;
Using ways with quite care.

Elusive are their discovery;
Seldom are their recovery;
O! O! I've a mountain to command;
Into the sea with my demand.

Frail is my faith;
From childhood since birth;
Like Peter sinking into the sea;
When Jesus, him walking on water, had to see.

As it comes, GODLY WORD, by hearing;
In those who are willing, and IT nearing;
No pleasure with GOD without it;
With a sigh of relief, I've a mountain to command.

POETIC FOOD SAFETY AND HYGIENE PROGRAMME
Amidst several problems;
Food inspectors think solemnly;
About food management;
Like its arrangement.

To prevent spoilage;
And the unnecessary disposal of food garbage;
forming part of environmental characteristics;
To be portrayed in statistics.

A difficulty still remains;
As earthly resources are limited;
To train every food handler
For targeting is the best idea.

Knowledge gap worsens the situation;
Requiring information, education and communication;
Through electronic and print media;
To prevent conditions like diarrhea;

A tool, to their addressing has come;
Thus, Food Safety and Hygiene Programme;
By conducting food premises Inspection;
Food handlers' testing, multisectoral collaboration;
And food safety and hygiene committee formation.

A poetic food safety and hygiene programme

OH! NO, NO, NOT AT ALL
Let's unite;
Altogether as a single unit;
To develop our nation;
Should laziness be our fashion?
Oh! No, no, not at all.

Let's be in real love;
Of a ring which is round;
To keep off enmity and hatred;
Should jealousy be our cartridge?
Oh! No , no, not at all.

Let's be time observant;
And punctuality compliant;
As it is in monetary terms;
Should we be caught in African time?
Oh! No, no, not at all.

Let's have a positive mindset;
Which is the fulcrum of development;
By teaching our young ones from youth;
Will they depart from it after full growth?
Oh! No, no, not at all.

All in all, let's fear GOD;
As HIS fear is wisdom and life of abundance;
Should we act against HIS guidance?
Oh! No, verily no, not at all.

A PARRYING PESTLE

A pestle, away my fortunes, it parries;
Like surface run off through the gullies;
Their realization, just about to attain;
Hit it hard, them away, now and again.

Works , it, out diligently against my destiny;
While exercising upon me mutiny;
Emasculated are my arms;
Self asking who I am.

May be tomorrow;
Anticipates, I, with sorrow;
As it parries away them continually;
Haunted, I, by it perpetually.

A pa-, par-, parrying pestle;
Screamed, I, like grasping the nettle;
Parried away is another basket of fortunes;
Approached, it, at the time opportune.

Dauntlessly and relentlessly, act do I
Waiting with faith, will I;
A parrying pestle shall instead be parried asunder;
Ha! A basket of fortunes on my verandah.
A pestle my fortunes, really, it parried away;

MY DEAR MUM

My dear mum! My dear mum!!
Irredeemable cost of care to me rendered;
By your protective and relentless deeds;
Showering upon my existing life span;
As an orchard with a watering cane.

My dear mum! My dear mum!!
A virtuous woman you are;
Gathering our food from afar;
For her house, she nourishes;
As hunger and malnutrition perishes.

My dear mum! My dear mum!!
Unexplainable love, to us, you illustrate;
As good conduct, to us, you demonstrate;
Like a vessel of advice, you act;
Full of reality and facts.

My dear mum! My dear mum!!
What an invaluable patience you possess?
Throughout my existence;
What is its foundation?
To infinity is my imagination.

My dear mum! My dear mum!!
This is my humble present;
May GOD have you abundantly blessed;
My dear Mum! My dear mum!!

IF SATAN, PHYSICALLY, EXISTED

If Satan existed physically;
Unimaginable, his appearance would be;
As he is an evil spirit;
Commonplace, he is;

Several questions, I pose;
No answer seems responded;
As he could, physically, be dealt with;
Futile, my imagination is.

Would his movements, limited, be?

\Would he speak to man as in Eden?
Would he transfigure into several forms?
Would he look attractive?
Would he still be a trickster?

In physical nature, act he;
Transfiguration, he can undergo;
An angel of light, he can pretend to be;
A father of lies, he will ever be.

In any form, he can be dealt with;
With CHRIST's sin healing blood, defeated he is;
To his operations, poisonous, it is;
By CHRIST, curse of death was conquered.

He loams around;
Whom he may devour, seeks he;
With his messengers' help;

AT THE TIP OF MY FINGERS

Keeping the law of GOD;
More precious than pure gold
Perish, the earth, will;
But the LAW is still;

Daily, upon it, meditate;
Life situations, to it, relate;
Trespasses, against it, repent;
Negligence, towards it, relent.

At the tip of my fingers;
Bound, it is, as symbolic figures;
Lest, forget I, the nature of my CREATOR;
WHO is the universe's MAKER.

Strength, it is, to your bones;
Health, it is, to your flesh;
Filled with plenty, your barns, will be;
Ways of pleasantness and peace, in it, are.

At ahe tip of my fingers, keep it, I.

UNRAVELLED TALENTS

O! O! Free! Priceless! Unraveled talents!
Embedded within, till present;
Undiscerned from the cradle to the grave;
Causing displeasure for HIS NAME's sake.

Failing to be LAW cautious;
Energetically being covetous;
Talent focus deviation, it becomes;
Like the whirl wind that never calms.

Back to ME unused, they return;
Angered is HIM in turn;
Unthankful attitude, to HIM, we demonstrate;
As HIS word, to us, it illustrates.

Shackled and locked up is our mindset;
Like sheep after the sunset;
Entangled in somebody's destiny;
Always we go astray.

Unraveled talents, really, there are.

FOOD TO MY SOUL

Hunger and thirst, chased away, they are;
Satisfied with food and drink, my body, them don't bear;
Lacking is food to my soul;
Like a carpenter without a saw.

Music, generally, it is referred to;
Spiritual music, specifically, attention pay I to;
My soul, soothes it;
As window panes wiped with windowlene.

To my soul's floor, acts it as a broom;
Sweeping away anguish and thoughts of doom;
As a consequence of, my past bad, reminiscing;
Which transpire in minutes.

Relaxed is my mindset;
As the sun's disappearance during the sunset;
Harvest of happiness, from it, emanates;
As springs of hope and peace, in it, are imminent.

Rebukes, it, my conduct;
As the fear of GOD is its product;
My heart, with it, is filled;
Displaced like water, evil, out is spilled.

Really, spiritual music is food to my soul.

THE GREATEST GEM IN CREATION
Troubled in my mind;
Prior to dine;
Lingering thoughts swirled;
As winds which ever whirled.

To unravel a mystery;
Seemingly to be imaginary;
About the greatest gem;
In creation as the theme.

Elusive is where to start;
As arrows missing targets in darts;
A meal for me on the table;
As my mind began, down, to settle;

Might it be food?
Or gold which is precious and good;
It could be life;
Priceless and out of sight.

Eureka, long at last;
Reminisced, I, of CHRIST;
Preaching about IT to that congregation;
As the most enduring Thing in creation.

Word is its unique name;
As GOD created the universe using the Same;
It was with GOD;
As it was also GOD;
For it was CHRIST;

THE POWER OF THREE

Mhu! Numbers!
Originating all from zeroes to nines;
Depicting quantity;
Complemented by quality.

With the HOLY TRINITY, begins it;
Composed of the FATHER, SON and the HOLY SPIRIT;
Three people survived from Sodom and Gomorrah;
Being Lot and his two daughters.

Executive, judiciary and parliament;
As the arms of the government;
Occurring in these days;
Divided into morning, afternoon and evening.

After three days, CHRIST resurrected;
And so was Jonah, from the fish, released;
In Gethsemane, took HE, three disciples;
As HE, Elijah and Moses, on that mountain glared.

On three crosses, crucified, were three men;
After three Peter's denials on that dawn;
To CHRIST's grave, three women brought spices;
Before HIS capture, prayed HE three times.

For three times, asked HE Peter's love;
Sold was HE for ten times three pieces;
10 times 3years, the onset of HIS ministry was;
11 times 3years was HIS death age.

3 eastern wise men, to HIM, presented three gifts;
With three creatures sin began;
Never got burnt, were Misheck, Shadrek and Abed-Nego;
For three times, Balaam beat that speaking donkey;
Endless the list is.
The power of three!

MY WORST ENEMY

Experiences of hatred;
Against me, they are kindled;
Verbally, expressed, they are.
As. Silently, the concerned act.

Tangibly or intangibly, exist they;
As my counselor says;
With stern admonition;
And avoid abomination.

Present, are they, internally or externally;
As the most dangerous enemy occurs internally;
Due to personal acts;
Oh! My worst enemy, really, I am.

UNTAMED TONGUE

Waking up in the morning;
Irritating is the tongue;
Troubled is the mind;
Compelled to talk, during day break, all kinds.

Speaking anyhow;
Social confusion created somehow;
As thought preceded by speech;
For none, me, beseech.

Negative consequences, from it, emanate;
Conflicts, gossips, idleness, e.t.c., in it, are imminent;
Like bush fires, spread, is false tale;
Character assassination overflows in his/her mental pail.

Dignity erosion, encountered by him/her, when acknowledged;
Like bare soil without vegetative cover;
A poor time planner, an individual becomes;
As the character never calms.
Untamed tongue, mostly, is counter productive.

BACK TO SQUARE ONE

In a battle field;
Against earthly troubles with a shield;
Retreat I to the starting line;
After attempted advances in a time;
Back to square one, the day's order is;

Problem solving tactics lacking;
Lacking are problem solving tactics;
As their knowledge gaps are usual characteristics;
Due to instructional negligence;
Or subsequent ignorance;
Back to square one, the day's order is.

Subsequent incapacitation and incapability;
Natural failures culminate into fallibility;
Pull somebody down syndrome taking its toll;
Inferiority complex, out in us, roll;
Back to square one, the day's order is.

Ba- Back! To square one, detest I ;
Naturally or intentionally, caused, it is;
From it, pending emancipation, must arise;
Satisfied with it, not, am I;
Back to square one must be erased.

IN HARMONY WITH NATURE

Man as an ecosystem's component;
To him, authority was dominant;
As GOD's creature;
In harmony with nature, existed he.

Set in, sin had;
Natural peace, to search for, got hard;
Imminent carelessness never got calm;
For ignorant/negligent, he had become;
In harmony with nature, had he never been.

Interrupted was natural balance;
Rendered was the ecosystem without solace;
Exerted is pressure on the environment;
Harmony between man and nature in disappointment;
In harmony with nature, cruelty inflicts he instead.

Serious environmental degradation;
Cruelty, to us, in reciprocation;
Reversal in harmonious consequences;
Extinction of natural systems/species;
In harmony with nature, backfired reactions, against us, are.

In harmony with nature;
Deem, us, for the future;
Peaceful existence and actions towards it;
Dream, us, with wits;
In harmony with nature, in harmony with man too.

LEARNING IT A HARD WAY

Difficulty in knowledge acquisition;
Complained, the learner, in repetition;
Airing, one's views, out;
Like tea, through the teapot's spout.

Disobedient to established standards;
As a commoner, being to laggards;
Subsequent ignorance also is its occurrence;
With inevitable coincidence.

Reversible are consequences;
As modified/redressed are changes with resilience;
Others, irreversible, they are;
Just behavioral changes occur.

Learning a hard way, an unwelcome encounter, really, it is.

UNFORSEEN DESTINY

Like moving through a tunnel;
In design of a funnel;
Channeling one's future;
In no foresight of its picture;
Through an unforeseen destiny, pass I.

Blinded to tomorrow;
Required is faith not sorrow;
In the hands of the CREATOR;
Put I everything, as my MAKER;
Through an unforeseen destiny, pass I .

For HIS NAME's sake;
HIS paths we take;
Due to personal desires;
Astray, we go, into mires;
Through an unforeseen destiny, pass we.

Imminent are streaks of doubt;
Fuzzy visions bubble out;
In a spirit of content;
Against us, nothing will contend;
Through an unforeseen destiny, pass we.

CONTACT AND DIALOGUE

Contact and dialogue;
Titled by an announcer at the prologue;
Of the presentation on the radio;
In design of a stereo.

Taking place between/among people;
Sharing ideas, either difficult or simple;
And also problem solving;
Which is involving.

Into play, it comes;
During confrontations, quarrels and strife;
As a result of opposing opinions;
To strike a mutual decision.

Fundamental results, brings it;
Peaceful idea sharing is in it;
Prevented are physical, psychological and economic damages.
Relationship restoration, it encourages;
Economic resource use;
Manifested as times pass.

Threats, the tool has;
Compromising characters, it, renders worse;
Towards it, avoid negligence;
About it, eliminate ignorance;
Contact and dialogue, an indispensable tool, really, it is.

POWERS I DON'T SEE

Struggle in the mental arena;
Of two powers, one unstable and the other serene;
Influencing one's behavior;
In dire need of the SAVIOR;
Both powers I don't see.

Dominating due to one's choice;
Unstable power controls in rejoice;
Bringing, its fruits, forth;
Unstable in nature and without truth;
It's just the power I don't see.

Without smell, they are;
Untouchably, they act;
Only through perception;
Or infinite conception;
Really, the powers I don't see;

Serene power in control!
From it, emanates peace and acts of moral;
Serene power in dominance;
As an individual enjoys solace;
But, it's the power I don't see.

OH! My mental sieve!
Infiltrate through the serene!
Expel out the unstable!
Permitting my heart, down, to settle;
OH! Still, these powers, I don't see.

BETTER DAYS ARE IMMINENT

After a toiling work;
Being sleep's enemy, mostly awake;
Struggling with strings of poverty;
Enjoyable is a solace, at last, with liberty;
For better days are imminent.

Acting with one accord;
While loosening its cords;
For its isolation from us;
Being, to us, a menace;
For better days are imminent.

Keeping our heads, just above the waters;
Mediocrity in our economic quarters;
Acting out of necessity not choice;
As mute is my voice;
For better days are imminent;

Bet-! Better days are imminent?
Oh! Oh! From us, how it emanate?
Broken into pieces, strings of poverty will be;
Meaningfully be as busy as a bee;
For better days are imminent.

A FIVE VOWEL CONVERSATION

Spenser and Joe in a spiritual conversation;
With facts and careful consideration;
Begins, it, with Spenser;
Speaking out his mind without censor;
Nature, by accident, it became;
Aaaa! Wrong information and is insane.

Joe, him, admonishes;
Whose intellectual stature, he has to polish;
Eeee! Intellectual vandalism;
Take life with spiritual mannerism;
Understand Spencer;
E! e! e! understand, I, it.

Iiiii! Lost in the jungle, I am;
Teach me, Joe, about that;
Everything, mysteriously planned and created, was;
The WORD, JESUS CHRIST, is its source;
II! i! i! what a great MAN is HE;
Living eternally till present?

Ooo!! That was blasphemy;
Challenging CHRIST as an enemy;
Repent now!
To HIM bow!
Forgiven will be your sins;
Covered, they will be, like water in tins.

Uh! What a gracious SAVIOR!

My spirit, solace, has found;
Like still waters sinking deep into the ground;
Worshipping HIM, always, will I;
With supplication, adoring HIM, will I be;

Ends a five vowel conversation.

NURTURING TALENTS

A special natural ability or skill;
Like rare species on a tourist destination hill;
Pouring out its uniqueness and splendor;
As sweet smelling flowers which are tender.

Manifested in an individual;
Whose unveiling is rapid or gradual;
Witnessed by the owner or contacts;
Appreciating or marveling at one's conduct.

Though, within us, it is embedded;
Diligently, it must be identified;
Its usage, thoroughly considered;
Lest it becomes withered.

Cherished, it must be;
Nurtured, always, it has to be;
As seedlings on a nursery;
With a well cleared boundary.

Protection from foes is a must;
As frivolity, complacency, recklessness, e.t.c. towering like a
mast;
Guarded, it should be, against covetousness;
For total seriousness.

THE START THAT WENT OFF

Usually eager for a new activity to start;
With all possibilities set apart;
Ignoring the impact of the setbacks.
Like chewing good mixed with rotten groundnuts.

In place were resources;
For prevention of poor performance;
For its completion was all hope;
Its realization seemed without any grope.

Suddenly occurred a turn around;
Appeared were setbacks in cyclical rounds;
Nose diving the start was;
As it crushed through the stagnation floors.

Extinct, the start had been;
Its existence out of scene;
Drained away were the resources;
Demotivation in the workplace.

On proper foundation, laid the start, should be;
After setbacks and possibilities, diligently, weighed;
In their sound combinations, prioritized;
That meaningful results must be materialized.

Disgraceful! Was that start that went off!

THE LINES THAT NEVER MEET

Into spirit, soul and body;
A complete person is molded;
In conflict are the desires of body and SPIRIT;
Being numerous in digits;
Like the parallel lines that never meet.

Eternal are Spiritual desires;
Mortal are carnal pleasures;
Incompatible are these forces;
As a rolling stone that grow no mosses;
Like parallel lines that never meet.

Peace and purity, by SPIRIT, brought forth;
Wickedness, by carnality, perverts the truth;
Lasting are spiritual fruits;
As if planted around springs;
Like parallel lines that never meet.

Never, never will they meet;
As, together, they don't fit;
Though, in a person;
Further apart, they are, like the earth and the horizon;
Like parallel lines that never meet.

THE INESCAPABLE THIN LINE

Walking along a line;
Likened to be six inches wide;
Between evil and good;
Stepped on by each foot;
Walking through an inescapable thin line, we are.

Tiring away on the way;
Choice struggle, rendering me to sway;
Towards either side;
Like a tourist without a guide;
Walking through an inescapable thin line, we are.

No average choice, the affair, is;
As one foot on the land and the other in the sea;
Just one choice suffices;
For one's life to sacrifice;
Walking through an inescapable thin line, we are.

UPHILL JOURNEY

The road to success;
Likened to a hill top with access;
Full of challenges along the way;
To be overcome without dismay.

Total determination, requires it;
Though, tiresome, it is;
Groping for the hill top;
Like grasshoppers that hop.

As dirty cleaned away by a mop;
So are obstacles with stern hope;
As preparations lead to good performance;
Always ready, must we, with endurance.

Success! Long at last!
Discipline being a must;
Obstacles forgotten;
Satisfaction and happiness begotten.

Uphill journey, eventually a reality.

DOWNHILL SPIRAL TRAIL

Normal life or situation;
Experienced without any complication;
In stability, by supporting figurative pillars;
Arranged, for mobility, like legs of caterpillars.

Sets in, complacency;
Loosened is normal constancy;
Gradual is the loss of control;
As along downhill trail, being spiral.

Figurative pillars out of order;
As normality begins to smoulder;
Restlessness and disorientation;
Like chaff moved by wind in rotations.

Downhill spiral, is the trail;
Compelling one to fail;
Ending up into trouble;
As challenges repeatedly double.

The downhill spiral trail, really is chaotic.

THE CONTAINER OF LIFE

How mysterious is the life's container?
Water, food, air and energy being its sustainers;
Of complex systems/processes, it is composed;
To various influences, it is exposed.

Its continuous, disjoined surface, marvel at, I;
With head, trunk and limbs, becomes it;
As a super machine, it functions;
Works, it, in an extraordinary fashion.

Being far more than a super high computer, its head is;
With touch and movement, the limbs provide it;
Fuel usage, in the trunk and cells, occurs;
As food consumption recurs.

Limited, it is, in existence;
As natural functions lose consistence;
Evaporated away is life;
Its subsequent degradation is nigh.

Hygienic/spiritual foods and knowledge, it, nourishes;
That it never perishes;
Physical exercises, it, build up;
Protected, it must be, from environmental mishaps.

In the container of life, safely dwells I .

IN HARMONY WITH NATURE

Man as an ecosystem's component;
To him, authority was dominant;
As GOD's creature;
In harmony with nature, existed he.

Set in, sin had;
Natural peace, to search for, got hard;
Imminent carelessness never got calm;
For ignorant/negligent, he had become;
In harmony with nature, had he never been.

Interrupted was natural balance;
Rendered was the ecosystem without solace;
Exerted is pressure on the environment;
Harmony between man and nature in disappointment;
In harmony with nature, cruelty inflicts he instead.

Serious environmental degradation;
Cruelty, to us, in reciprocation;
Reversal in harmonious consequences;
Extinction of natural systems/species;
In harmony with nature, backfired reactions, against us, are.

In harmony with nature;
Deem, us, for the future;
Peaceful existence and actions towards it;
Dream, us, with wits;
In harmony with nature, in harmony with man too.

MY FATHER, RESPECT YOU, I

My father, several services by you, rendered;
That our lives may not be endangered;
As family head, yourself, you present;
Like church's head, when CHRIST will descend;
Really, father, respect you, I.

For your family, real love, you show;
Like CHRIST for the church, its seeds HE sows;
Symbolizing the FATHER of heavenly kingdom;
Whose fear is wisdom;
Of course, father, respect you, I.

Act you, like a vessel of advice;
From which we draw guidance and good acts;
For our daily life's application;
And subsequent, on several issues, qualification;
Definitely, father, respect you, I.

My father, always stay blessed;
Let us not, up, be messed;
By earthly temptation;
As we act against your admonition;
Undoubtedly, father, respect you, I.

The Enigma Of Poetry-Volume One is a poetic book consisting of poems of various types. The types are as follows:

Spiritual Issues:: This document is portraying the issues of spirituality. It is talking about how you should attain the status of Christianity. This starts by believing in jesus Christ and accepting m as one's personal saviour.

We are living in the world of conflicting choices.

Nature: Some poems are expressing the issues of the creation of nature and the human impact on mother nature with her reciprocate consequences.

Human personalities and behaviours:These are being featured in certain poetic pieces. They are both bad and good personalities or behaviours.

The journey through life: The journey through life is unforeseable.

We pass through hard and pleasant situations. All in all, we should give thanks to God Almighty for the precious gift of life which HE gives us daily. We should learn to enjoy our life continually despite having several challenges along our respective destinies.

This has been just to mention a few of the issues this book holds.

Read, underatand, enjoy and share the information therein.

Thanks

]